Wednesday

MARVIN BELL

Wednesday

Selected Poems 1966 - 1997

Salmonpoetry

Published in 1998 by
Salmon Publishing Ltd,
Cliffs of Moher, Co. Clare

A catalogue record for this book is available from the British Library.

The Arts Council
An Chomhairle Ealaíon

Salmon Publishing gratefully acknowledges the financial assistance of The Arts Council.

ISBN 1 897648 94 4 Softcover

Cover artwork by Austin Carey
Cover design by Brenda Dermody of Estresso
Set by Siobhán Hutson
Printed by Betaprint, Clonshaugh, Dublin 17

Other Books by Marvin Bell

Ardor (The Book of the Dead Man, Vol. 2) [1997]

The Book of the Dead Man (Vol. 1) [1994]

A Marvin Bell Reader: Selected Poetry and Prose [1994]

Iris of Creation [1990]

New and Selected Poems [1987]

Drawn by Stones, by Earth, by Things that Have Been in the Fire [1984]

Old Snow Just Melting: Essays and Interviews [1983]

Segues: A Correspondence in Poetry (with William Stafford) [1983]

These Green-Going-to-Yellow [1981]

Stars Which See, Stars Which Do Not See [1977]

Residue of Song [1974]

The Escape into You [1971]

A Probable Volume of Dreams [1969]

Things We Dreamt We Died For [1966]

To Dorothy, Nathan, Jason, Leslie, Colman, and Aileen

To my mother, to the memory of my father,
and to my sister Ruby

To Frank DiGangi and Carole Worthington

Acknowledgments

The forty poems in section one are reprinted from the following collections: *Things We Dreamt We Died For* (The Stone Wall Press, 1966); *A Probable Volume of Dreams* (Atheneum, 1969); *Stars Which See, Stars Which Do Not See* (Atheneum, 1977); *These Green-Going-to-Yellow* (Atheneum, 1981); *Drawn by Stones, by Earth, by Things that Have Been in the Fire* (Atheneum, 1984); *New and Selected Poems* (Atheneum, 1987); *Iris of Creation* (Copper Canyon Press, 1990); and, *A Marvin Bell Reader* (Middlebury College Press/University Press of New England, 1994).

Dead Man poems # 1, 13, 15, and 23 appeared in *The Book of the Dead Man* (Copper Canyon Press, 1994). Dead Man poems #35, 42, 58, and 63 appeared in *Ardor: The Book of the Dead Man, Vol. 2* (Copper Canyon Press, 1997). 'Sounds of the Resurrected Dead Man's Footsteps' #4 and #23 appeared in *Shenandoah*; #6 appeared in *Prairie Schooner*; and, #13 appeared in *Green Mountains Review*.

Contents

Author's Preface

If a selection of poems written over thirty years must inevitably blur the discrete nature of each previous collection, and if it seems to its author as if each poem has been flung into critical hyperspace, untethered to the conventions and experiments of its age, there is the compensation that some few poems might yet survive apart from time and coordinates. In reading poetry, as in reading its familiar cousin, philosophy, we fancy that a vision need not proceed from ripe to rotten.

The writing self has another point of view. It fancies that new work grows out of the great entropic humus. It seeks an art made from fallibility, a poetry that defeats mere learning. Some of us favor such an art; we desire it; we may even need it. For us, going our own way has depended on a buried compass.

The forty poems that appear in the first part of this selection are taken from books published from 1966 through 1994. The next twelve are from an ongoing project known as 'the dead man poems.' Numbers 1-33 of this work-in-progress appeared in 1994 in *The Book of the Dead Man*, and numbers 34-70 in 1997 in *Ardor* (The Book of the Dead Man, Vol. 2). From the preface to Volume 1:

'Before the birth of the Dead Man, it was not possible to return. It was not possible, it was pre-conceptual, it was discretionary to the point of chaos and accident to return, since of course there was nowhere yet to return to. Since the birth of the Dead Man, however, it is possible, even likely, that one may return. From the future, one walks ever more slowly into the past.'

I wish to thank Ben Howard and Jessie Lendennie, who foresaw and oversaw, respectively, the publication of this selection of poems, and Gerard Donovan, who took me to see the Cliffs of Moher.

M. B.

He Had a Good Year

while he was going blind. Autumnal light
gave to ordinary things the turning
beauty of leaves, rich with their losing.
A shade of yellow, that once stood opaque
in the rainbow of each glitzy morning,
now became translucent, as if the sun
broke against his own window. As for white,
it was now too much of everything,
as the flat deprivations of the colour black
moved farther away: echoes of a surface
unseen and misremembered. I must tell you
how he managed as the lights went slowly out
to look inside the top glow of each object
and make in his mind a spectrum of inner
texture, of an essence isolate from the
nervous trembling of things struck by light.
'Ah, if God were only half the man he is,'
he said, 'he would see things this way.'

Wednesday

Gray rainwater lay on the grass in the late afternoon.
The carp lay on the bottom, resting, while dusk took shape
in the form of the first stirrings of his hunger,
and the trees, shorter and heavier, breathed heavily upwards.
Into this sodden, nourishing afternoon I emerged,
partway toward a paycheck, halfway toward the weekend,
carrying the last mail and holding above still puddles
the books of noble ideas. Through the fervent branches,
carried by momentary breezes of local origin,
the palpable Sublime flickered as motes on broad leaves,
while the Higher Good and the Greater Good contended
as sap on the bark of the maples, and even I
was enabled to witness the truly Existential where it loitered
famously in the shadows as if waiting for the moon.
All this I saw in the late afternoon in the company of no one.

And of course I went back to work the next morning. Like you,
like anyone, like the rumoured angels of high office,
like the demon foremen, the bedevilled janitors, like you,
I returned to my job – but now there was a match-head in
    my thoughts.
In its light, the morning increasingly flamed through
    the window
and, lit by nothing but mind-light, I saw that the horizon
was an idea of the eye, gilded from within, and the sun
the fiery consolation of our nighttimes, coming far.
Within this expectant air, which had waited the night indoors,
carried by – who knows? – the rhythmic jarring of brain tissue

by footsteps, by colours visible to closed eyes, by a music
in my head, knowledge gathered that could not last the day,
love and error were shaken as if by the eye of a storm,
and it would not be until quitting that such a man
might drop his arms, that he had held up all day since the dew.

Two Pictures of a Leaf

If I make up this leaf
in the shape of a fan, the day's cooler
and drier than any tree. But if
under a tree I place before me
this same leaf as on a plate,
dorsal side up and then its ribs
set down like the ribs of a fish –
then I know that fish are dead to us
from the trees, and the leaf
sprawls in the net of fall to be
boned and eaten while the wind gasps.
Ah then, the grounds are a formal ruin
whereon the lucky who lived
come to resemble so much that does not.

Trees as Standing for Something

1

More and more it seems I am happy with trees
and the light touch of exhausted morning.
I wake happy with her soft breath on my neck.
I wake happy but I am happier yet.
For my loves are like the leaves in summer.
But oh!, when they fall, and I wake with a start,
will I feel the sting of betrayal and ask, What is this
love, if it has to end, even in death,
or if one might lose it even during a life?
Who will care for such a thing?
Better to cut it down where it stands.
Better to burn it, and to burn with it,
than to turn around to see one's favourite gone.

2

It began when they cut down the elm and I let them.
When the corkscrew willow withered and I said nothing.
Then when the soft maple began to blow apart,
when the apple tree succumbed to poison,
the pine to a matrix of bugs, the oak to age,
it was my own limbs that were torn off, or so it seemed,
and my love, which had lived through many storms,
died, again and again. Again and again, it perished.
What was I to say then but Oh, Oh, Oh, Oh, Oh!
Now you see a man at peace, happy and happier yet,
with her breath on the back of his neck in the morning,
and of course you assume it must always have been this way.
But what was I to say, then and now, but Oh! and Oh! Oh!

The Self and the Mulberry

I wanted to see the self, so I looked at the mulberry.
It had no trouble accepting its limits,
yet defining and redefining a small area
so that any shape was possible, any movement.
It stayed put, but was part of all the air.
I wanted to learn to be there and not there
like the continually changing, slightly moving
mulberry, wild cherry and particularly the willow.
Like the willow, I tried to weep without tears.
Like the cherry tree, I tried to be sturdy and productive.
Like the mulberry, I tried to keep moving.
I couldn't cry right, couldn't stay or go.
I kept losing parts of myself like a soft maple.
I fell ill like the elm. That was the end
of looking in nature to find a natural self.
Let nature think itself not manly enough!
Let nature wonder at the mystery of laughter.
Let nature hypothesise man's indifference to it.
Let nature take a turn at saying what love is!

Unless It Was Courage

Again today, balloons aloft in the hazy *here*,
three heated, airy, basket-toting balloons,
three triangular boasts ahead against the haze
of summer and the gravity of onrushing fall –
these win me from the wavery *chrr*-ing of locusts
that fills these days the air between the trees,
from the three trembly outspreading cocoons hanging
on an oak so old it might have been weighed down
by the very thought of hundreds of new butterflies,
and from all other things that come in threes
or seem to be arranged. These *are* arranged,
they are the perfection of mathematics as idea,
they have lifted off by making the air greater –
nothing else was needed unless it was courage –
and today they do not even drag a shadow.

It was only a week ago I ran beneath one.
All month overhead had passed the jetliners,
the decorated company planes, the prop jobs
and great crows of greed and damage (I saw one
dangle a white snake from its bill as it flew),
and all month I had looked up from everywhere
to see what must seem from other galaxies
the flies of heaven. Then quickly my chance came,
and I ran foolish on the grass with my neck bent
to see straight up into the great resonant cavity
of one grandly wafting, rising, bulbous, whole
balloon, just to see nothing for myself. That
was enough, it seemed, as it ran skyward and away.
There I was, unable to say what I'd seen.
But I was happy, and my happiness made others happy.

To No One in Particular

Whether you sing or scream,
the process is the same.
You start, inside yourself,
a small explosion, the difference
being that in the scream
the throat is squeezed so that
the back of the tongue
can taste the brain's fear.
Also, spittle and phlegm
are components of the instrument.
I guess it would be possible
to take someone by the throat
and give him a good beating.
All the while, though, some fool
would be writing down the notes
of the victim, underscoring
this phrase, lightening this one,
adding a grace note and a trill
and instructions in one of those languages
revered for its vowels.
But all the time, it's consonants
coming from the throat.
Here's the one you were throttling,
still gagging out the guttural ch –
the throat-clearing, Yiddish ch –
and other consonants spurned by
opera singers and English teachers.
He won't bother you again.
He'll scrape home to take it out
on his wife, more bestial consonants
rising in pitch until spent.

Then he'll lock a leg over her
and snore, and all the time
he hasn't said a word we can repeat.
Even though we all speak his language.
Even though the toast in our throats
in the morning has a word for us –
not at all like bread in rain,
but something grittier in something
thicker, going through what we are.
Even though we snort and sniffle,
cough, hiccup, cry and come
and laugh until our stomachs turn.
Who will write down this language?
Who will do the work necessary?
Who will gag on a chickenbone
for observation? Who will breathe perfectly
under water? Whose slow murder
will disprove for all time
an alphabet meant to make sense?
Listen! I speak to you in one tongue,
but every moment that ever mattered to me
occurred in another language.
Starting with my first word.
To no one in particular.

The Uniform

Of the sleeves, I remember their weight, like wet wool,
on my arms, and the empty ends which hung past my hands.
Of the body of the shirt, I remember the large buttons
and larger buttonholes, which made a rack of wheels
down my chest and could not be quickly unbuttoned.
Of the collar, I remember its thickness without starch,
by which it lay against my clavicle without moving.
Of my trousers, the same – heavy, bulky, slow to give
for a leg, a crowded feeling, a molasses to walk in.
Of my boots, I remember the brittle soles, of a material
that had not been made love to by any natural substance,
and the laces: ropes to make prisoners of my feet.
Of the helmet, I remember the webbed, inner liner,
a brittle plastic underwear on which wobbled
the crushing steel pot then strapped at the chin.
Of the mortar, I remember the mortar plate,
heavy enough to kill by weight, which I carried by rope.
Of the machine gun, I remember the way it fit
behind my head and across my shoulder blades
as I carried it, or, to be precise, as it rode me.
Of tactics, I remember the likelihood of shooting
the wrong man, the weight of the rifle bolt, the difficulty
of loading while prone, the shock of noise.
For earplugs, some used cigarette filters or toilet paper.
I don't hear well now, for a man of my age,
and the doctor says my ears were damaged and asks
if I was in the Army, and of course I was but then
a wounded ear drum wasn't much in the scheme.

What Songs the Soldiers Sang

Those with few images, lyrics
in which doing and undoing
prevailed, there were conclusions
and many epithets.
To hell with what it might look like!
The idea of breakfast, to take one
example, was a favourite
in the evenings. Also,
the way fields shut down,
and the weight of the equipment.
In choruses full of objects
nothing civilian moved
but loud young men bent on silence
and backbreaking labours.
It was natural to welcome them
with triumphal marches.
Many would return in halves.
The songs, too, about their singing, are lies.
The truth is that some songs were obscene
and that there were no words for others.

Theory of Relativity (Political)

When I was young, dreaming of luminescent escapades set against the light of a great pearl hung in a sky that would otherwise be black, as if it were the one thing certain to survive the overwhelming forces of the tide of an invisible sea, I once thought of becoming a policeman but gave it up and became something else. Then one day the sea rose up and heaved itself from the sky, collapsing in exhaustion on the earth where it lay trying to catch its breath. From this I learned that the fiercest incandescence can be swallowed by accident if an open maw goes by, swimming or flying. From the cultivated moon we must shift our attention to a speck of sand hung in an eye from which tears have fallen onto the earth and lie sighing. If we are going to be the world's policemen, we had better train for microcosms and the faces of wristwatches, for the damage one does in a small area just by turning around can cause tremors that travel by root and branch and spread like cracks in the crust of the desert. I and my countrymen, being patriotic, listen for organic pressures building under the surface, and in any event one does not want to play God when God plays God.

Interview

Do you believe that actors are dumb? Writers?

Which of the following do you think are the dumbest:
actors, writers, policemen, firemen, hunters,
or generals?

How about social workers, teachers, doctors, realtors?

Fat people, prisoners, the poorly dressed, the visibly
impoverished?

The sick, the old, the lovesick, the lonely; those who
make mistakes in public, those who apologise,
the silent, the talkative?

Do you approve of torture under any circumstances? Which?

What form of torture do you favour – physical,
psychological, etc.?

Do you approve or disapprove of euthanasia? For others?
For yourself?

What form of euthanasia do you prefer? For others?
For yourself? Is cost an issue? Would you prefer that
your death be carried out by someone other than
yourself? Close friends? Family members? If a doctor
shows up bearing a lethal injection, would you feel it
improper to refuse?

Which bodily functions do you find the most embarrassing
to discuss?

Are there things you would say to one sex but not to
the other?

Stars Which See, Stars Which Do Not See

They sat by the water. The fine women
had large breasts, tightly checked.
At each point, at every moment,
they seemed happy by the water.
The women wore hats like umbrellas
or carried umbrellas shaped like hats.
The men wore no hats and the water,
which wore no hats, had that well-known
mirror finish which tempts sailors.
Although the men and women seemed at rest
they were looking toward the river
and some way out into it but not beyond.
The scene was one of hearts and flowers
though this may be unfair. Nevertheless,
it was probable that the Seine had hurt them,
that they were 'taken back' by its beauty
to where a slight breeze broke the mirror
and then its promise, but never the water.

The Hole in the Sea

It's there
in the hole of the sea
where the solid truth lies,
written and bottled,
and guarded by limp-
winged angels –
one word under glass,
magnified by longing
and by the light tricks
of the moving man
in the moon.
Nights, that word shows,
up from the bottle,
up through the water,
up from the imaginable.
So that all who cannot
imagine, but yearn toward,
the word in the water,
finding it smaller
in the hole in the sea,
rest there. If no one
has drowned quite
in the hole of the sea,
that is a point
for theology. 'Blame God
when the waters part,'
say sailors and Hebrews;
blame God, who writes us,
from His holy solution,
not to be sunk,
though all our vessels

convey black messages
of the end of the world.
So goes the story,
the storybook story, so goes
the saleable story:
Courage is in that bottle,
the driest thing there is.

The Mystery of Emily Dickinson

Sometimes the weather goes on for days
but you were different. You were divine.
While the others wrote more and longer,
you wrote much more and much shorter.
I held your white dress once: 12 buttons.
In the cupola, the wasps struck glass
as hard to escape as you hit your sound
again and again asking Welcome. No one.

Except for you, it were a trifle:
This morning, not much after dawn,
in level country, not New England's,
through leftovers of summer rain I
went out rag-tag to the curb, only
a sleepy householder at his routine
bending to trash, when a young girl
in a white dress your size passed,

so softly!, carrying her shoes. It must be
she surprised me – her barefoot quick-step
and the earliness of the hour, your dress –
or surely I'd have spoken of it sooner.
I should have called to her, but a neighbour
wore that look you see against happiness.
I won't say anything would have happened
unless there was time, and eternity's plenty.

Written During Depression: How to Be Happy

To be happy,
a man must love death
and failure. Then,
however great the flash
of this moment or that bit
of life's work, there
will come always another moment
to be appreciated because
fading or crumbling. If,
however, a man loves
life, there can be no end to it,
nor hope. If a man loves
reason, eventually he
will find none. If he loves
the interest of others,
he will be made to apologise
continually for his own being.
If he loves form, all
that he does or knows will
come, not to nothing, but
to that other possibility
of meaninglessness: everything.
That is why 'the shape of things
to come' is a phrase littered with
tracks into the bush
where the pure primitive
is a headhunter's delusion,
and why, my dear, I love you.

Trinket

I love watching the water
ooze through the crack in the fern pot,
it's a small thing

that slows time
and steadies
and gives me ideas of becoming

having nothing to do
with ambition or even reaching,
it isn't necessary at such times

to describe this,
it's no image for mean keeping,
it's no thing that small

but presence.
Other men look at the ocean,
and I do too,

though it is too many
presences for any
to absorb.

It's this other,
a little water, used, appearing
slowly around the sounds

of oxygen and small frictions,
that gives the self
the notion of the self

one is always losing
until these tiny embodiments
small enough to contain it.

What Is There

When the grass, wet and matted,
is thick as a dry lawn is not,
I think of a kind of printing –
a page at a time, and the thick
paper hung up to dry, its
deep impressions filled and shapely
where ink is held and hardens.

And I wonder then at the underside
of those damp sheets of grass –
the muddy blood of those buried
coming up into the flattened green
as I press it underfoot, and pass,
and the sun drawing moisture
until we accept what is written there.

Treetops

My father moves through the South hunting duck.
It is warm, he has appeared
like a ship, surfacing, where he floats, face up,
through the ducklands. Over the tops
of trees, duck will come, and he strains
not to miss seeing the first of each flock,
although it will be impossible to shoot one
from such an angle, face up like that
in a floating coffin where the lid obstructs
half a whole view, if he has a gun.
Afterlives are full of such hardships.

One meets, for example, in one's sinlessness,
high water and our faithlessness,
so the dead wonder if they are imagined
but they are not quite.

How could they know we know
when the earth shifts deceptively
to set forth ancestors to such pursuits?
My father will be asking, Is this fitting?
And I think so – I, who, with the others,
coming on the afterlife after the fact
in a dream, in a probable volume, in a
probable volume of dreams, think so.

These Green-Going-to-Yellow

This year,
I'm raising the emotional ante,
putting my face
in the leaves to be stepped on,
seeing myself among them, that is;
that is, likening
leaf-vein to artery, leaf to flesh,
the passage of a leaf in autumn
to the passage of autumn,
branch-tip and winter spaces
to possibilities, and possibility
to God. Even on East 61st Street
in the blowzy city of New York,
someone has planted a gingko
because it has leaves like fans like hands,
hand-leaves, and sex. Those lovely
Chinese hands on the sidewalks
so far from delicacy
or even, perhaps, another gender of gingko –
do we see them?
No one ever treated us so gently
as these green-going-to-yellow hands
fanned out where we walk.
No one ever fell down so quietly
and lay where we would look
when we were tired or embarrassed,
or so bowed down by humanity
that we had to watch out lest our shoes stumble,
and looked down not to look up
until something looked like parts of people
where we were walking. We have no

experience to make us see the gingko
or any other tree,
and, in our admiration for whatever grows tall
and outlives us,
we look away, or look at the middles of things,
which would not be our way
if we truly thought we were gods.

Things We Dreamt We Died For

Flags of all sorts.
The literary life.
Each time we dreamt we'd done
the gentlemanly thing,
covering our causes
in closets full of bones
to remove ourselves forever
from dearest possibilities,
the old weapons re-injured us,
the old armies conscripted us,
and we gave in to getting even,
a little less like us
if a lot less like others.
Many, thus, gained fame
in the way of great plunderers,
retiring to the university
to cultivate grand plunder-gardens
in the service of literature,
the young and no more wars.
Their continuing tributes
make them our greatest saviours,
whose many fortunes are followed
by the many who have not one.

A Primer about the Flag

Or certain ones. There are Bed & Breakfast flags.
They fly over vacancies, but seldom
above full houses. Shipboard, the bridge can say
an alphabet of flags. There are State flags
and State Fair flags, there are beautiful flags
and enemy flags. Enemy flags are not supposed
to be beautiful, or long-lasting. There are flags
on the moon, flags in cemeteries, costume flags.
There are little flags that come from the barrel
of a gun and say, 'Bang.' If you want to have
a parade, you usually have to have a flag
for people to line up behind. Few would
line up behind a small tree, for example,
if you carried it at your waist just like a flag
but didn't first tell people what it stood for.

A Man May Change

As simply as a self-effacing bar of soap
escaping by indiscernible degrees in the wash water
is how a man may change
and still hour by hour continue in his job.
There in the mirror he appears to be on fire
but here at the office he is dust.
So long as there remains a little moisture in the stains,
he stands easily on the pavement
and moves fluidly through the corridors. If only one
cloud can be seen, it is enough to know of others,
and life stands on the brink. It rains
or it doesn't, or it rains and it rains again.
But let it go on raining for forty days and nights
or let the sun bake the ground for as long,
and it isn't life, just life, anymore, it's living.
In the meantime, in the regular weather of ordinary days,
it sometimes happens that a man has changed
so slowly that he slips away
before anyone notices
and lives and dies before anyone can find out.

The Politics of an Object

The banana is stronger than the human head in the following ways: those fine threads that wave from the top knot are harder to break than hair. Should you pick one up, you cannot resist peeling it: it will have done to it what it was born to have done to it. As for endurance and sacrifice: while thousands of well-muscled labourers did not survive the cheap labour of imperialism in their republics, and others died with their mouths stuffed full of money, the banana hung on, gathering potassium. It knew the future, it knew its history, it was prepared for bruises. I have gathered the small colourful stickers applied one to a bunch until now they cover the wooden arms of the chair where I often linger in the kitchen to chat with my wife. The bananas don't last long, eaten or not. But each of the tiny stickers, each company logo, stays in place incorruptibly, and, though I am but one man, without a plan, I am keeping their names in mind. So you see? A banana is superior to a human head because it gives up without a fight. And still there is a future.

The Pill

The pill, in the pill bottle, humming like a wheel at rest, confident that the time must come when it will control the future and distance unravel to the end of time – this small round package of power, this force for lingering life or lingering death, this salt for the soul, this spice with roots in antiquity – this coated equation smaller than a fingertip embodies and contains you. And who gave it that right, who harnessed chemistry and put *things* in charge? We demand to know. We intend to hold them responsible: death would be too good for them. The search begins in the home, it begins just behind the mirror: there, in the bathroom cabinet, are the innocuous masters of our lives – the toothpaste, the deodorant, the shampoo. Someone has decreed that we should not remain during the days those briny, glistening starfish as which we crawled the bottoms of seas to suck up the smallest, reddest forms of life. It is not so bad to be in the air now, routine to live as two beings: one in the light, the other just beneath the light-tight skin of sleep. But to be the third thing: the creature that was given, by mistake, the demented brain, and now must absorb with flaccidity the daily dose of electricity that will prolong its self-knowledge. For it is one thing to be alive – the grass is alive, the pea and the potato grow, and microscopic algae stain with their living bodies the snow of the coldest regions – and another thing to *know* that one is alive. Where in philosophy was it decided that, if it is good to be able to choose, it is twice good to realise it? The argument that once raged inside the spiral corridors of a nautilus, at a depth a human being could only imagine, sings all around us like wind in the alleys, like city water in the sewers. We have not been shocked enough yet. We are not yet ready. Great areas of our brains still lie dormant like the liquid-carved underside of a coral reef. The debate rages in words and gestures. Sparks open up new hallways between logic and instinct. But it is in the dormant regions of the brain, the resonant cavities of absolute not-knowing, that life is closest to the source of life. A whole brain like that is like a head carried in on a plate. For a moment, it is one thing that looks like another thing. For a moment, everyone in the room could have sworn that it could see them, and that it blinked.

White Clover

Once when the moon was out about three-quarters
and the fireflies who are the stars
of backyards
were out about three-quarters
and about three-fourths of all the lights
in the neighbourhood
were on because people can be at home,
I took a not so innocent walk
out among the lawns,
navigating by the light of lights,
and there there were many hundreds of moons
on the lawns
where before there was only polite grass.
These were moons on long stems,
their long stems giving their greenness
to the centre of each flower
and the light giving its whiteness to the tops
of the petals. I could say
it was light from stars
touched the tops of flowers and no doubt
something heavenly reaches what grows outdoors
and the heads of men who go hatless,
but I like to think we have a world
right here, and a life
that isn't death. So I don't say it's better
to be right here. I say this is where
many hundreds of core-green moons
gigantic to my eye
rose because men and women had sown green grass,
and flowered to my eye in man-made light,
and to some would be as fire in the body
and to others a light in the mind
over all their property.

Nature

A hand that tries to shake a hand,
an ear pressed against a silver railroad track,
in a place one goes to be alone
called by various names for parts of the body.
Waiting for this, waiting for that.
Swept by the penetrant odour of choked lilies
and the smoke of dark clouds.
Alone by virtue of a garden. And then
with all five senses about to expire,
suddenly a wedding of male and female
in pools of electro-chemical memory
that existed before dawn,
before thick and thin, before the dead thought.
Earth of dusk. Earth of the belly. Earth of the breast.
And heaven the heaven of a slash
that wakes the sea.
All that is better, all that is worse,
whatever is half-formed,
which is to say everything born one of two parents,
every living thing turned round in the cave,
unable to distinguish the unlit road
from the bright slash in the sky,
shall be set free to roam
to find a husband or a wife
with whom to ruminate
on the messages in the footprints of ants and flies
and on the rights of others, too, who live
a few hours only or part of a day
without once hearing a rooster
scare away an angel.

Long Island

The things I did, I did because of trees,
wildflowers and weeds, because of ocean and sand,
because the dunes move about under houses built on stilts,
and the wet fish slip between your hands back into the sea,
because during the War we heard strafing across the Bay
and after the War we found shell casings with our feet.
Because old tires ringed the boat docks,
and sandbags hung from the prows of speedboats,
and every road in every country ends at the water,
and because a child thinks each room in his house big,
and if the truth be admitted, his first art galleries
were the wallpaper in his bedroom and the carlights
warming the night air as he lay in bed counting.

The things I did, I counted in wattage and ohms,
in the twelve zones that go from pure black to pure white,
in the length of the trumpet and the curves of the cornet,
in the cup of the mouthpiece. In the compass and protractor,
in the perfect bevelled ruler, in abstract geometry,
and if the truth be known, in the bowing of cattails
he first read his Heraclitus and in the stretching box turtle
he found his theory of relativity and the gist of knowledge.
He did what he did. The action of his knee in walking
was not different from the over-stretching of an ocean wave,
and the proofs of triangles, cones and parallelograms
were neither more nor less than the beauty of a fast horse
which runs through the numbers of the stopwatch and
    past the finish.

The things I counted, I counted beyond the finish,
beyond rolling tar roadways that squared the fields,
where I spun on the ice, wavered in fog, sped up or idled,
and, like Perry, like Marco Polo, a young man I saw
alone walk unlit paths, encircled by rushes
and angry dogs, to the indentations of his island.
And if the truth be told, he learned of Columbus,
of Einstein, of Michelangelo, on such low roads and
    local waters.
Weakfish hauled weakening from the waters at night,
and the crab rowing into the light, told him in their way
that the earth moved around the sun in the same way,
with the branched mud-print of a duck's foot to read,
and life in the upturned bellies of the fishkill in the creek.

An Old Trembling

Often one wonders what the snake does all day in its pit
to so successfully keep away hands
and be left alone like a solitary zipper
encircling some space from which it has squeezed out all
the light
it would seem,
as if no other creature could so love the dark during the day.
And everyone knows about the kiss of the snake.
And everyone knows about the eyes of the snake.
In its mouth is the blue light of old milk.
On its tongue is a map of red rivers.
It knows your body, your own body, like its own.
It begins with your foot, lurking in a boot,
and ends in the venomous sweat of the heart
if you bother it. But whoever leaves alone
whatever in nature wishes not to be disturbed,
he or she will seem like a god,
so unlike a human being,
even to a snake.

Victim of Himself

He thought he saw a long way off the ocean
cresting and falling, bridging the continents,
carrying the whole sound of human laughter
and moans – especially moans, in the mud of misery –
but what he saw was already diluted, evaporating,
and what he felt were his teeth grinding
and the bubbles of saliva that broke on his tongue.

He was doomed to be a victim of himself.
He thought he saw, in the future, numberless, cavernous
burials – the outcome of plagues, of wars,
of natural disasters created by human beings –
but what he saw was already faded, disintegrating,
and what he felt was the normal weakness displayed
by droopy eyes and muscles that bleated meekly.

He thought he saw from Earth up to the stars
and from any one moment back to the hour of his birth
when desire produced, in the slush of passionate tides,
a citizen of mud and ash, of lost light and dry beds,
but what he saw was already distorted, moving away,
and what he felt was a sense of loss that so often
he had been at peace in her arms when he did not
intend to be.

The Nest

The day the birds were lifted from my shoulders,
the whole sky was blue, a long-imagined effect
had taken hold, and a small passenger plane
was beating the earth with its wings
as it swung over the bean fields toward home.
A fat car barely travelled a narrow road
while I waited at the bottom of a hill.
People around me were speaking loudly
but I heard only whispers, and stepped away.

You understand, I was given no choice.
For a long time, I was tired of whatever it was
that dug its way into my shoulders for balance
and whispered in my ears, and hung on for dear life
among tall narrow spaces in the woods
and in thickets and crowds, like those of success,
with whom one mingles at parties and in lecture halls.
In the beginning, there was this or that . . .
but always on my shoulders that which had landed.

That was life, and it went on in galleries
and shopping plazas, in museums and civic centres,
much like the life of any responsible man
schooled in the marriage of history and culture
and left to learn the rest at the legs of women.
In furtive rooms, in passing moments, the sea
reopened a door at its depth, trees spoke
from the wooden sides of houses, bodies became
again the nests in the naked tree.

After that, I was another person,
without knowing why or how, and after that,
I lived naked in a new world where the sun
broke through windows to grasp entire families
and crept between trees to wash down streets
without disturbing any object, in a world
where a solitary kiss blew down a door.
The day the birds were lifted from my shoulders,
it killed me – and almost cost me a life . . . .

Comb and Rake

The comb that we love, of all combs,
is a rake through our private beach,
giving a voice through missing teeth
to all the things one hopes to find in the sand
next to horseshoes, aluminum tabs,
and sand ants thrilled by the sight of a claw.

The rake that we love, of all rakes,
is a comb through our private grove,
singing at perfect intervals
of all the things one hopes to be divine,
here, among human tongues rusting in fire,
bearing the singed hair and beard.

Of all names, the name we most love
mocks an unsaid name we did not love –
in the smallest possible space,
cast upon a screen encircled by a naked moon
at the centre of a solar system
where there is only you and me and someone else.

Eastern Long Island

Beach grass tangled by wind – the sound rushes
to every nautical degree –
here are torn memories of inlets and canals,
of ponds, bays, creeks, coves, spits and sandbars,
coastal moons and skies, tidal clumps of tiny crabs
that couldn't keep up, seaweed fixed
to stones looking like the heads of Chinese sages,
all criss-crossing the sundial of my dreams.

I dream more when the meteors come –
Earth's face slipping through a comet's tail –
reminder that we steer an unmarked channel,
buoyless, sounding the vacancy of space
where water turns
to take back what it said and deposit on the shore
the exhausted sailor, his tired, complaining boat,
and the wrack of salt water pouring through the slats.

Wasn't anything to be done. Where ships foundered,
where pilgrims settled and pioneers set off,
now contaminant plumes propose
marriage to the aquifer, this being the way it was
when the shark lost teeth to the incoming tide,
and those legs that covet the tide line
were torn from the armoured, methodical crab,
and the gull grabbed off the fish closest to the top.

Wasn't anything to be done – not then
when rapture simmered underwater, and we played
adulthood, taking sea horse and starfish,
nor later when the fishermen
followed their catch to deeper water,
leaving a stain that coated rocks and weeds
and seemed to be of a shade containing
its own shadow, an undulation in the channel.

Time has not ended. Yet already it is a struggle
to brush away the first few flecks
starlight lent this crystalline surface, then mute.
Earth's voice, a harmony begun in molten rumble,
rose through wash of water and rush of air
to the high pitch of grass blade and ether light.
Those first bits of impurity, that were to ruin
our diamond in the making, at first barely marked it.

I still love the radiance of a dim storm building
out where the tide seems to reverse and the sea vibrate,
puzzling perhaps to fresh eyes yet unfazed
by salt wells rising beneath these beds of clay.
At the tide line a fringe of seaweed keeps time,
and wind-whipped sand opaques our cottage windows.
By the boat ramp, disgorged clam shells await
reclamation by the proximate meek, who shall inherit.

Drawn by Stones, by Earth, by Things that Have Been in the Fire

I can tell you about this because I have held in my hand
the little potter's sponge called an 'elephant ear.'
Naturally, it's only a tiny version of an ear,
but it's the thing you want to pick up out of the toolbox
when you wander into the deserted ceramics shop
down the street from the cave where the fortune-
    teller works.
Drawn by stones, by earth, by things that have been in
    the fire.

The elephant ear listens to the side of the vase
as it is pulled upwards from a dome of muddy clay.
The ear listens to the outside wall of the pot
and the hand listens to the inside wall of the pot,
and between them a city rises out of dirt and water.
Inside this city live the remains of animals,
animals who prepared for two hundred years to be clay.

Rodents make clay, and men wearing spectacles make clay,
though the papers they were signing go up in flames
and nothing more is known of these long documents
except by those angels who divine in our ashes.
Kings and queens of the jungle make clay
and royalty and politicians make clay although
their innocence stays with their clothes until unravelled.

There is a lost soldier in every ceramic bowl.
The face on the dinner plate breaks when the dish does
and lies for centuries unassembled in the soil.
These things that have the right substance to begin with,
put into the fire at temperatures that melt glass,
keep their fingerprints forever, it is said,
like inky sponges that walk away in the deep water.

Ending with a Line from Lear

I will try to remember. It was light.
It was also dark, in the grave. I could feel
how dark it was, how black it would be
without my father. When he was gone.
But he was not gone, not yet. He was only
a corpse, and I could still touch him
that afternoon. Earlier the same afternoon.
This is the one thing that scares me:
losing my father. I don't want him to go.
I am a young man. I will never be older.
I am wearing a tie and a watch. The sky,
gray, hangs over everything. Today
the sky has no curve to it, and no end.
He is deep into his mission. He has business
to attend to. He wears a tie but no watch.
I will skip a lot of what happens next.
Then the moment comes. Everything, everything
has been said, and the wheels start to turn.
They roll, the straps unwind, and the coffin
begins to descend. Into the awful damp.
Into the black centre of the earth. I
am being left behind. The centre of my body
sinks down into the cold fire of the grave.
But still my feet stand on top of the dirt.
My father's grave. I will never again.
Never. Never. Never. Never. Never.

The Last Thing I Say

to a thirteen-year-old sleeping,
tone of an angel, breath of a soft wing,
I say through an upright dark space
as I narrow it pulling the door
sleepily to let the words go surely into
the bedroom until I close them in
for good, a nightwatchman's-worth
of grace and a promise for morning
not so far from some God's first notion
that the world be an image by first light
so much better than pictures of hope
drawn by firelight in ashes,
so much clearer, too, a young person
wanting to be a man might draw one finger
along an edge of this world and it
would slice a mouth there
to speak blood and then should he put that wound
into the mouth of his face,
he will be kissed there and taste
the salt of his father as he lowers
himself from his son's high bedroom
in the heaven of his image of
a small part of himself and sweet dreams.

To an Adolescent Weeping Willow

I don't know what you think you're doing,
sweeping the ground. You
do it so easily, backhanded, forehanded.
You hardly bend. Really, you sway.
What can it mean
when a thing is so easy?

I threw dirt on my father's floor.
Not dirt, but a chopped green
dirt which picked up dirt.

I pushed the pushbroom.
I oiled the wooden floor of the store.

He bent over and lifted the coal
into the coalstove. With the back of the shovel
he came down on the rat just topping the bin
and into the fire.

What do you think? – Did he sway?
Did he kiss a rock for luck?
Did he soak up water
and climb into light and turn and turn?

Did he weep and weep in the yard?

Yes, I think he did. Yes,
now I think he did.

So Willow, you come sweep my floor.
I have no store.
I have a yard. A big yard.

I have a song to weep.
I have a cry.

You who rose up from the dirt,
because I put you there
and like to walk my head in under
your earliest feathery branches –
what can it mean
when a thing is so easy?

It means you are a boy.

Poem after Carlos Drummond de Andrade

'It's life, Carlos.'

It's life that is hard: waking, sleeping, eating, loving,
working and dying are easy.
It's life that suddenly fills both ears with the sound of
that symphony that forces your pulse to race and
swells your heart near to bursting.
It's life, not listening, that stretches your neck and opens
your eyes and brings you into the worst weather of
the winter to arrive once more at the house where
love seemed to be in the air.

And it's life, just life, that makes you breathe deeply, in
the air that is filled with wood smoke and the dust of
the factory, because you hurried, and now your lungs
heave and fall with the nervous excitement of a leaf
in spring breezes, though it is winter and you are
swallowing the dirt of the town.
It isn't death when you suffer, it isn't death when you
miss each other and hurt for it, when you complain
that isn't death, when you fight with those you love,
when you misunderstand, when one line in a letter or
one remark in person ties one of you in knots, when
the end seems near, when you think you will die,
when you wish you were already dead – none of that
is death.
It's life, after all, that brings you a pain in the foot and a
pain in the hand, a sore throat, a broken heart,
a cracked back, a torn gut, a hole in your abdomen,
an irritated stomach, a swollen gland, a growth, a
fever, a cough, a hiccup, a sneeze, a bursting blood
vessel in the temple.

It's life, not nerve ends, that puts the heartache on a pedestal and worships it.
It's life, and you can't escape it. It's life, and you asked for it. It's life, and you won't be consumed by passion, you won't be destroyed by self-destruction, you won't avoid it by abstinence, you won't manage it by moderation, because it's life – life everywhere, life at all times – and so you won't be consumed by passion: you will be consumed by life.

It's life that will consume you in the end, but in the meantime . . .
It's life that will eat you alive, but for now . . .
It's life that calls you to the street where the wood smoke hangs, and the bare hint of a whisper of your name, but before you go . . .

Too late: Life got its tentacles around you, its hooks into your heart, and suddenly you come awake as if for the first time, and you are standing in a part of the town where the air is sweet – your face flushed, your chest thumping, your stomach a planet, your heart a planet, your every organ a separate planet, all of it of a piece though the pieces turn separately, O silent indications of the inevitable, as among the natural restraints of winter and good sense, life blows you apart in her arms.

Short Version of Ecstasy

Up-welling of forces, serums and fevers,
tracking conduits of emotion,
following the longing of waist, elbows and knees
to crease to and fro, to be wind and wild
as any petal of in-growing rose bud in storm.
Until, and not until, each still quivering tendon
flops its last and pales;
until, and not until, something of a trance or sleep
blankets the bed; until, and not until, a dozen instances
lift and collapse in a headless consciousness
of release, and the gorged blood descends
by an intermittent elevator of stems,
will the lovers let go of themselves or each other.

Can they stand to get up now? So far have they slid
from the inflated lungs of love,
from the gasping expectation and the drag
of skin on skin as they sank after having held up
their coming, they who moved as one
raw from the separate rates of their falling,
such a distance have they gone, up and down then,
that each may recall the middle of the story
only by its frame. After the event,
the photo of the lover expels no scent, no invitation
sufficient to satisfy. It is truly over until,
and only until, some hidden residue of passion
sways into being, wanting to die.

To Dorothy

You are not beautiful, exactly.
You are beautiful, inexactly.
You let a weed grow by the mulberry
and a mulberry grow by the house.
So close, in the personal quiet
of a windy night, it brushes the wall
and sweeps away the day till we sleep.

A child said it, and it seemed true:
'Things that are lost are all equal.'
But it isn't true. If I lost you,
the air wouldn't move, nor the tree grow.
Someone would pull the weed, my flower.
The quiet wouldn't be yours. If I lost you,
I'd have to ask the grass to let me sleep.

If I Had One Thing to Say

I see words effaced in the footprints of the conquered,
slowly sinking into the earth in a round sort
of way, indirect, like sunlight at night, and I see
the speeches of the conquerors preserved on paper,
hurried to a lead mine in the mountains and buried
deeper than atomic mushrooms, insulated
from firestorm and radiation and residue even if
the world has to wait ten thousand years for Adam.

I see grass growing rapidly in those footprints,
and the earth curving in space, and the lean of all
that holds on, from the laughter of the lone coyote
high up in the night to the wishbone of the kill,
hung head down to drain and every part used
and remembered as long as song, deep as prayer,
with the words handed down through centuries
of naming and telling and there's always another Adam.

I see dust made of the fibres of grass, of paper,
from the rubbings of the dirt, the pumice of dead bone,
from the cells of our skin migrating to the surface,
and I see that the dust will never settle, neither
in time nor space, but in the rain of a thousand centuries
many things clear now to us – impulses at the core –
may come to rest in the form of a thought, and this
may be the way it is already: the way it was for Adam.

Poems from

'The Book of the Dead Man'

'Ardor'

&

'Sounds of the Resurrected Dead Man's Footsteps'

Live as if you were already dead.

– Zen admonition

The Book of the Dead Man (#1)

1. About the Dead Man

The dead man thinks he is alive when he sees blood in
his stool.
Seeing blood in his stool, the dead man thinks he is alive.
He thinks himself alive because he has no future.
Isn't that the way it always was, the way of life?
Now, as in life, he can call to people who will not answer.
Life looks like a white desert, a blaze of today in which
nothing distinct can be made out, seen.
To the dead man, guilt and fear are indistinguishable.
The dead man cannot make out the spider at the centre
of its web.
He cannot see the eyelets in his shoes and so wears
them unlaced.
He reads the large type and skips the fine print.
His vision surrounds a single tree, lost as he is in a forest.
From his porcelain living quarters, he looks out at a
fiery plain.
His face is pressed against a frameless window.
Unable to look inside, unwilling to look outside, the
man who is dead is like a useless gift in its box waiting.
It will have its yearly anniversary, but it would be wrong
to call it a holiday.

2. More About the Dead Man

The dead man can balance a glass of water on his head
without trembling.
He awaits the autopsy on the body discovered on the
beach beneath the cliff.
Whatever passes through the dead man's mouth is expressed.
Everything that enters his mouth comes out of it.
He is willing to be diagnosed, as long as it won't disturb
his future.
Stretched out, he snaps back like elastic.
Rolled over, he is still right-side-up.
When there is no good or bad, no useful or useless, no
up, no down, no right way, no perfection, then okay
it's not necessary that there be direction: up is down.
The dead man has the rest of his life to wait for colour.
He finally has a bird's-eye view of the white hot sun.
He finally has a complete sentence, from his head to his feet.
He is, say, America, but he will soon be, say, Europe.
It will be necessary merely to cross the ocean and pop up
in the new land, and the dead man doesn't need
to swim.
It's the next best thing to talking to people in person.

The Book of the Dead Man (#13)

1. About the Dead Man and Thunder

When the dead man hears thunder, he thinks someone
 is speaking.
Hearing the thunder, the dead man thinks he is being
 addressed.
He thinks he is being addressed because the sound
 contains heat and humidity – or groaning and salivation.
Isn't that always the way with passionate language – heat
 and humidity?
The dead man passes burning bushes and parting seas
 without inner trembling, nor does he smear his door
 with blood.
The dead man can only be rattled physically, never
 emotionally.
The dead man's neuroses cancel each other out like a
 floor of snakes.
He is the Zen of open doors, he exists in the zone of the
 selfless, he has visions and an ear for unusual music.
Now he can hear the swirling of blood beneath his heartbeat.
Now he can fall in love with leaves – with the looping
 lift and fall of love.
Naturally, the dead man is receptive, has his antennas
 out, perches on the edge of sensitivity to receive the
 most wanton prayer and the least orderly of wishes.
To the dead man, scared prayer isn't worth a damn.
The dead man erases the word for God to better
 understand divinity.
When nothing interferes, nothing interrupts, nothing
 sustains or concludes, then there's no need to
 separate doing from not-doing or to distribute the
 frequencies of the thunder into cause and effect.
The dead man speaks God's language.

2. More About the Dead Man and Thunder

The dead man counts the seconds between lightning
and thunder to see how far he is from God.
The dead man counts God among his confidants:
they whisper.
The dead man hears the screams of roots being nibbled
by rodents.
He notes the yelps of pebbles forced to manoeuvre and
of boulders pinned into submission.
He feels the frustration of bodily organs forced to be quiet.
He thinks it's no wonder the sky cries and growls when
it can.
The dead man's words can be just consonants, they can
be only vowels, they can pile up behind his teeth like
sagebrush on a fence or float like paper ashes to the
top of fathomless corridors, they can echo like wind
inside a skull or flee captivity like balloons that have
met a nail.
The dead man serves an indeterminate sentence in an
elastic cell.
He hears a voice in the thunder and sees a face in the
lightning, and there's a smell of solder at the junction
of earth and sky.

The Book of the Dead Man (#15)

1. About the Dead Man and Rigor Mortis

The dead man thinks his resolve has stiffened when the
ground dries.
Feeling the upward flow of moisture, the dead man
thinks his resolve has stiffened.
The dead man's will, will be done.
The dead man's backbone stretches from rung to rung,
from here to tomorrow, from a fabricated twinge to
virtual agony.
The dead man's disks along his spine are like stepping
stones across a lake, the doctor told him 'jelly
doughnuts' when they ruptured, this is better.
The dead man's hernial groin is like a canvas bridge
across a chasm, the doctor said 'balloon' when they
operated, this is better.
The dead man's toes are like sanded free forms and his
heels are as smooth as the backs of new shoes,
the doctor said 'corns' when they ached, this is better.
The dead man's eyes are like tiny globes in water, continental
geographies in microcosm, all the canyons are visible,
now washed of random hairs that rooted, now free of
the strangulated optics of retinal sense, this is better.
All the dead man's organs, his skin, muscles, tendons,
arteries, veins, valves, networks, relays – the whole
shebang hums like a quickly deserted hardware store.
To the dead man, a head of cabbage is a forerunner
of nutrients.
The dead man's garden foreshadows the day it is to be plowed
under, agriculture being one of the ancient Roman
methods for burying the Classics, the other was war.
No one can argue with the dead man, he brooks no
interference between the lightning and ground, his
determination is legendary.

2. More About the Dead Man and Rigor Mortis

You think it's funny, the dead man being stiff?
You think it's an anatomically correct sexual joke?
You think it's easy, being petrified?
You think it's just one of those things, being turned to stone?
Who do you think turns the dead man to stone anyway?
Who do you think got the idea first?
You think it's got a future, this being dead?
You think it's in the cards, you think the thunder spoke?
You think he thought he was dead, or thought he
  fancied he was dead, or imagined he could think
  himself dead, or really knew he was dead?
You think he knew he knew?
You think it was predetermined?
You think when he stepped out of character he was different?
What the hell, what do you think?
You think it's funny, the way the dead man is like
  lightning, going straight into the ground?
You think it's hilarious, comedy upstanding, crackers to
  make sense of?

The Book of the Dead Man (#23)

1. About the Dead Man and His Masks

When the dead man thinks himself exposed, he puts on
  a mask.
Thinking himself exposed, the dead man puts on a mask.
Before he needed a mask, he wore his medals on his
  chest and his heart on his sleeve.
The dead man wears the mask of tomfoolery, the mask of
  assimilation, the mask of erasure, the scarred mask,
  the teen mask, the mask with the built-in *oh*,
  the laughing mask, the crying mask, the secretive
  mask, the telltale mask, and of course the death mask.
The dead man's masks are as multifarious as the wiles of
  a spider left to work in the bushes.
To the dead man, a spider's web is also a mask, and he
  wears it.
The trail of a slug is a mask, and the vapours from
  underground fires are a mask, and the dead light of
  sunset is a mask, and the dead man wears each of them.
The dead man curtained off the world, now everything
  between them is a mask.
He weaves masks of sand and smoke, of refracted light
  and empty water.
The dead man takes what the world discards: hair and
  bones, urine and blood, ashes and sewage.
The dead man, reconstituted, will not stay buried,
  reappearing in disguises that fool no one yet cast doubt.
He comes to the party wearing the face of this one or
  that one, scattering the shadows as he enters.
When there is no one face, no two faces, no fragility of
  disposition, no anticipation, no revelation at
  midnight, then naturally years pass without anyone
  guessing the identity of the dead man.
It is no longer known if the dead man was at the funeral.

2. More About the Dead Man and His Masks

The dead man's mask prefigures all *ism*'s such as surrealism, patriotism, cronyism, futurism, Darwinism, barbarism, dadaism, Catholicism, Judaism, etc.

Many of the dead man's masks are museum pieces: final expressions from Death Row, those startled at the last second in Pompeii or Dresden or Hiroshima, faces surprised in the trenches, the terror of furnaces and lime, a look formed from suffocation or lengthy bleeding or embalming.

The dead man apologises for leaving a sewing machine and an umbrella on the operating table.

The dead man catalogs war memorials, potter's fields, he takes stock of undiscovered suicides, pseudonyms and all instances of anonymity.

The dead man's masks are composed of incongruous materials accidentally combined and are as rare and wild as certain edible fungi that closely resemble poisonous mushrooms.

He doffs his hat to long hair, moustaches and beards, but does not give himself away.

He greets the grieving, the relieved, the startled, the victimised and the triumphant without letting on.

The dead man's hands are twice as expressive in gloves, his feet deprived of their arches gain momentum in shoes, and his mask shields him from those who wish to trade knowledge for truth.

The dead man's first mask was a hand over his mouth.

The Book of the Dead Man (#35)

1. About the Dead Man and Childhood

In an evening of icicles, tree branches crackling as they
break frozen sap, a gull's bark shattering on snow, the
furnace turned down for the night, the corpse air
without exits – here the dead man reenters his fever.
The paste held, that was dry and brittle.
The rotting rubber band stuck to the pack of playing
cards to keep it together.
In the boy's room, the balsa balanced where there had
once been glue.
Recognition kept its forms in and out of season.
Why not, then, this sweaty night of pursuit?
He has all of himself at his disposal.
He has every musical note, every word, though certain
notes of the piano have evaporated.
Shall he hear them anyway?
The dead man's boyhood home withholds from its current
occupants the meaning of desecration, nor shall they
be the destroyers of the past in their own minds.
You too have seen anew the giant rooms of the little
house in which you were a child.
You have seen the so-heavy door that now barely resists
a light hand.
You have walked down the once endless corridors that
now end abruptly.
Were you so small then that now you are in the way?
You too sat at the impossibly high kitchen table with
your feet dangling, drawn down by the heavy shoes.
All this and more the dead man remembers the
connective quality of.
In those days, there was neither here nor now, only there
and the time it would take to reach it.

2. More About the Dead Man and Childhood

After Adam ate the apple, there was one more, and then
one more . . . .
After Orpheus looked back, there was another and
another . . . .
The dead man discerns betwixt and between, he knows
mania and depression, he has within him the two
that make one, the opposites that attract, the
summer pain and the winter pain.
He walks both the road of excess and the least path,
and lives most in the slow-to-ripen spring and
extended autumn.
The dead man does not come when called but tries to
hit a baseball in the dusk.
He does not yet know he wants to ride the horse that
took the bit in its mouth.
He lives in the attic and the big closet where the radio
parts and the extra glassware hold their codes.
He is the initiate.
He feigns nothing, he has nothing else in mind, later he
will be charged with having been a boy.
Even now, in May and September he feels the throbbing
tissue of that fallow world from which he was forced
to be free.
The dead man in adulthood knows the other side, and
he winces at the fragility of the old songbooks, taped
and yellowed, held there in time.

The Book of the Dead Man (#42)

1. About the Dead Man's Not Telling

The dead man encounters horrific conditions infused
with beauty.
He looks and sees, dare you see with his unblinkered eyes.
He sniffs and ingests, dare you do the same as he.
He hears and feels, dare you secure such stimuli and
endure the heart.
He sets foot on the anomalies, he traverses the interior
laden with the screams of witnesses underfoot.
He walks among the pines crackling with the
soon-to-be-broken backs of new life.
He freely rests among the appetites of the unsatisfied.
He bites off the head of the Buddha.
The dead man has seen bad Buddhahood.
He has doubled back, he has come around, he has cut
across, he has taken the long shortcut.
What is out there, that germinates?
The dead man knows that there is no luck but dumb
luck, no heart that will not skip, no pulse that does
not race.
Things go, time goes, while the dead man stays.

2. More About the Dead Man's Not Telling

Has not the dead man asked a basic question?
Did he not lie in the crib like a question mark without
a sentence?
Did he not encode the vitality of roots, the beauty of
leaves, the kinetics of branches, the rapture of the sun,
the solace of the moon, even the hollow that shapes
the seed?
The dead man is the one to ask when there is asking.
Those who invest in the past or future shall forfeit the
dead man's objectivity, his elasticity strung from
down-and-dirty to up-and-ready.
When the oracle spoke, the dead man listened like a shell.
When the quixotic signalled from the wood, the dead
man grasped the new life that needed no more
plasma than the dew.
How comely the horrific consequences, how amiable the
gorgeous advantage of the newly born.
Things go, time goes, but the dead man goes nowhere
without you.
You who told him know what is on the dead man's mind.
You at the fringe, the margin, the edge, the border,
the outpost, the periphery, the hinterland, you at the
extremity, you at the last, counterpoised, have caught
the inference.
The dead man counts by ones and is shy before your
mildest adoration.

The Book of the Dead Man (#58)

1. About the Dead Man Outside

They came to the door because he was small or went to
some church or other or was seen in the company of
girls or boys.
Well, he was small and went to synagogue and didn't
know what to make of it.
They said he was from some tribe, but he didn't
understand it.
They acted as if they knew what they were doing.
They were the executioners of brown eyes and brown
hair, and he happened to have both.
Well, he said, and they went away before he awoke.
They were a dream he was having before he became the
dead man.
Today the dead man lives where others died.
He passes the crematoriums without breathing.
He enters the pit graves and emerges ashen or lime-laced.
He shreds the beautiful tapestries of history and hangs in
their place the rough shirts and dank pants forsaken
at the showers, and the tiny work caps.
He mounts the hewn chips of shoesoles, the twisted
spectacles, the tortured belts and suspenders,
the stained handkerchiefs.
Here, he says, is history, maternity, inheritance.

2. More About the Dead Man Outside

Let none pardon the Devil lest he have to begin again.
Let no one weep easily, let no one build portfolios of
disaster snapshots or record the lingo of the know-
betters, let no one speak who has not considered
the fatalities of geography.
The dead man does not suffer skinheads lightly, their
evil is legion.
With an olive branch, he whips the villains into a frenzy
of repentance.
The dead man tattoos the war criminals with the numbers.
The dead man wonders what America would be like
if every war were a wall engraved with the names of
the lost.
Well, they said, he was from some tribe or other, and he
didn't understand it.
When the dead man was a dead child, he thought as a child.
Now the dead man lives that others may die, and dies
that others may live.
Let the victims gather, the dead man stays on the outside
looking in.
Let the saved celebrate, the dead man stands distant, remote.
The dead man listens for the sound of Fascist boots.
They will be going again to his grave to try to cut down
his family tree.
This time the dead man will see them in Hell.

The Book of the Dead Man (#63)

1. About the Dead Man and Anyway

The dead man has up-the-stairs walking disorder.
He has one-foot-in-front-of-the-other indisposition and
other aspects of the wistful.
He has over-the-hillitis, the past-one's-prime predicament
of week-old celery or last year's universal theory.
The dead man has a pox, a condition, an affliction,
the usual entropic timing, the sudden parsimony of a
reformed spendthrift, all of it born of the purest,
simplest love: gratitude for having been.
What if the dead man's love were less, would that make
your pear wrinkle?
What if the dead man's truth were unsaid, would that
cause you to kiss yourself down there?
Come on, come off it, be upstanding, it's not all fruits
and vegetables, peaches and cream, rubber chickens
or joy buzzers.
The dead man never said he wouldn't die.
Anyway, the dead man is too alive to have been dead all
this time.
The dead man is the light that was turned on to study
the dark.
Where there is no more nonetheless, no before or after,
no henceforth or regardless, then the dead man in
his infirmity, deformity, and prolonged ability
overlaps his beloved in riotous whatchamacallit.
The dead man's language for love is largely blue-collar
whatchamacallit.

2. More About the Dead Man and Anyway

The dead man rubs salt in his wound anyway.
When the dead man finds in himself a hollow, he fills it
with salt anyway.
A little torture is breathtaking for as long as the dead man
can hold his breath.
The discomfort that will not let the dead man sit still is
transformed into curiosity by late night abandon.
The beauty of the horrific is bled of its human cost by
the long night of shaking.
The dead man, after long silence, sings his way through
the graveyards.
If there is any way to change pigskin to silk, the dead man
will find it.
Anyway, he has only one or two lives to give for his country.
He has only himself and his other self.
The dead man will not be countenanced or counterfeited,
he will not be understood by the merely reasonable,
he will not bleed his wounds of their hideous glamour
and come up pristine.
Those who would slightly reorganise the bones will find
their vanity unrewarded.
Those who would take the dead man's head away will lose
themselves in the topography of his skull.
The dead man stands for what things are, not what you
call them.
The dead man stands for living anyway.

Sounds of the Resurrected Dead Man's Footsteps (#4)

1. Fly, Fleece and Tractor

Legs arrayed, a spider observes me from the juncture of
wall and ceiling.
Little sunspot, unmoved by the rustle of a writer's clothes,
undisturbed by the passing locomotive saying 'Q,' 'Q.'
They all come to passing grief who ride these walls.
They perish by degrees who deny the wolf.
They are ground underfoot who fuss instead of running.
After insect-killing season, there comes the machinery,
then the corn upstanding and the animals grown
to harvest.
Then again the machinery.
He had been indoors, who planned to go outside.

2. Syringe, Cloak and Elevator

In a planting field, a tractor bears down on the evidence.
It does not feel the modernist division of mind and body.
Like liquid within a syringe, some people need a push to
go out.
Elsewhere, they who deny evil are covered by goodness
and must suffer.
Those who cannot go forward and backward must go up
and down.
He was farming, who was taken to the hospital.
The long winter was of thunder snow, and the spring
cacophony was of the wind and the almanac, and the
silence is the quiet of being watched.
One last late-night toot from the pantheistic locomotive,
then the owls.

Sounds of the Resurrected Dead Man's Footsteps (#6)

1. Skulls

Oh, said a piece of tree bark in the wind, and the night froze.
One could not have foreseen the stoppage.
I did not foresee it, who had expected a messiah.
No one had yet dared say that he or she was it – target
  or saviour.
In the slippage between time and the turning planet,
  a buildup of dirty grease made movement difficult.
Time slowed down while events accelerated.
The slower the eye moved, the faster events went past.
The raping and pillaging over time became one
  unending moment.
Nazis, who would always stand for the crimes of culture,
  clustered in public intersections, awaiting deliveries.
The masses would turn in the Jews.
From the officers' quarters could be heard the beautiful
  Schubert.
And in the camp there was the grieving tenor of the cantor.
The one rose and the other sank.
Today, one can stroll in the footsteps of those who
  walked single file from this life.
Often I stand in the yard at night expecting something.
Something in the breeze one caught a scent of as if a
  head of hair had passed by without a face.
Whatever happens to us from now on, it will come up
  from the earth.
It will bear the grief of the exterminated, it will lug itself
  upwards.
It will take all of our trucks to carry the bones.
But the profane tattoos have been bled of their blue by
  the watery loam, additives for worms.
Often I stand in the yard with a shovel.

2. Skulls

I am the poet of skulls without why or wherefore.
I didn't ask to be this or that, one way or another, just a young man of words.
Words that grew in sandy soil, words that fit scrub trees and beach grass.
Sentenced to work alone where there is often no one to talk to.
The poetry of skulls demands complicity of the reader, that the reader put words in the skull's mouth.
The reader must put water and beer in the mouth, and music in the ears, and fan the air for aromas to enter the nostrils.
The reader must take these lost heads to heart.
The reader must see with the eyes of a skull, comb the missing hair of the skull, brush the absent teeth, kiss the lips and find the hinge of the tongue.
Yes, like Hamlet, the Jew of Denmark before Shakespeare seduced him.
It is the things of the world which rescue us from the degradations of the literati.
A workshirt hanging from a nail may be all the honesty we can handle.
I am beloved of my hat and coat, enamoured of my bed, my troth renewed each night that my head makes its impression on the pillow.
I am the true paramour of my past, though my wife swoons at the snapshots.
Small syringe the doctor left behind to charm the child.
Colourful *yarmulke* that lifted the High Holy Days.

Sounds of the Resurrected Dead Man's Footsteps (#13)

1. Millennium

Like trying to pour entropy through a funnel.
The devilish moment, the thought that a ceremony
might make of one second something so illuminating
it would forever define us.
The illusion that a hand holding another hand is
attached to it.
Nothing I say or do.
This here means right now, rigorous as it is to be here
now, not there then.
One respects Miss Stein for avoiding the future.
Then there is the flashbulb that gets in one's eyes.
The mercury ascends in the thermometer, then bumps
on down.
Where were you when the world changed?
In southern Australia where the time zone was half-an-
hour ahead.
Thus, poetry without reference to time: *i.e.*, he has an
artificial heart but he still feels love.
Poetry regional within the body.
The mind always half-an-hour behind.
A sundial cannot be read under a Bo tree.
Your hand in mine on the midnight in question
crystallised the moment, or was it tears?

2. Posterity

The all-inclusive later, after you have read the piece
about now.
After the bawling is over, beyond contretemps, past
knowledge of mishaps.
Then's beyond.
But you want to know ahead of time – does she, will I,
will it keep?
Or not.
Throws a stone at a tree and, if it hits, the best is yet to be.
Throws a stone at a tree and, if it misses, throws another.
Did you act out such childhood rituals also?
Draws a line in the dirt before he beheads the chicken.
Keeps an umbrella in the car so it won't rain.
Recognition of hazards and safe areas.
Careful with mirrors, shies from reflective surfaces,
smiles at the camera.
A catalog of traits, survival skills, mannerisms and
customs, a complete list of instinctual responses and
reflexes, an inventory of do's and don'ts.
Nothing left to chance in the attempt to influence posterity.
That is, nothingness is left to chance, the chips fall
where they may, and the outcome remains unknown.
Quantum mechanics: a new generation redefines normalcy.
The seers rewinding their watches, the clairvoyants
squinting.
Shuffling the Tarot, recasting the *I Ching*, wrinkling
the lifeline, envisioning happenstance, charting
chaos, counting butterflies.
The new scythe swinging through poetry may or may not
have been honed.
My goal to be better than dirt.

Sounds of the Resurrected Dead Man's Footsteps (#23)

1. Baby Hamlet

Be that as it may, it may be that it is as it will be.
His word a sword without a hiss.
Cruelly, the son obliged to sacrifice himself to a feud.
On the Feast of the Angel of Consumption and Death.
We move through time beset by indecision.
Thus, events occur while waiting for the news.
Or stuck in moral neutral.
The Nazis willing to let aid enter the Camps if those
 bringing it swore not to help the prisoners escape.
The hopeless pacifism of those who promised.
The Platonic ideal carried to its logical inconclusion.
The heroes those who lied to the Third Reich.
Otherwise, the world stands caught between Hamlet
 and Ophelia.
Ophelia's dress a dead ringer for beauty.

2. The Play within the Play

Hamlet a man asked to die now.
Madness to try to make sense of a father's ghost.
To know one lives yet may not.
To imbibe a poison over time – wishing to be, yet consigned.
And the work details, the meagre rations, the Motherland.
Destined to clog the machinery of the State with one's body,
    Nazis the masters of whitewash.
Fairy dust rising from lime shovelled into the grave.
Poems and post-mortems a struggle with Danish
    collaboration.
Hamlet a play of ones foreshadowing a time of millions.
Hamlet addressing a skull the poet speaking to the dead.
Bones the bloodless gray of ancient manuscripts.
The eyes marbles clicking in their pockets.
Hamlet done to death with his head in his hands.